Whispers of the Soul

Sarah EllisonFlake

Published by Kristy S. Flake, 2024.

WHISPERS OF THE SOUL

First edition. February 2, 2024.

ISBN: 979-8224288052

Written by Sarah EllisonFlake.

Table of Contents

As I sit here and write this dedication I am filled with so many emotions and an overflow of gratitude. My book Whispers of the Soul would never been completed if it wasn't for my twins, I love you Kristopher & Kiaya. Since the day ya'll were born, ya'll have been my inspiration. This is my way of expressing my love for you both.

To my PapaBear this is my way of telling you thanks for your patience. You've got to have nerves of steel. I love you, without your ironclad patience and encouragement, this wouldn't been possible at all. Thank You Mine!

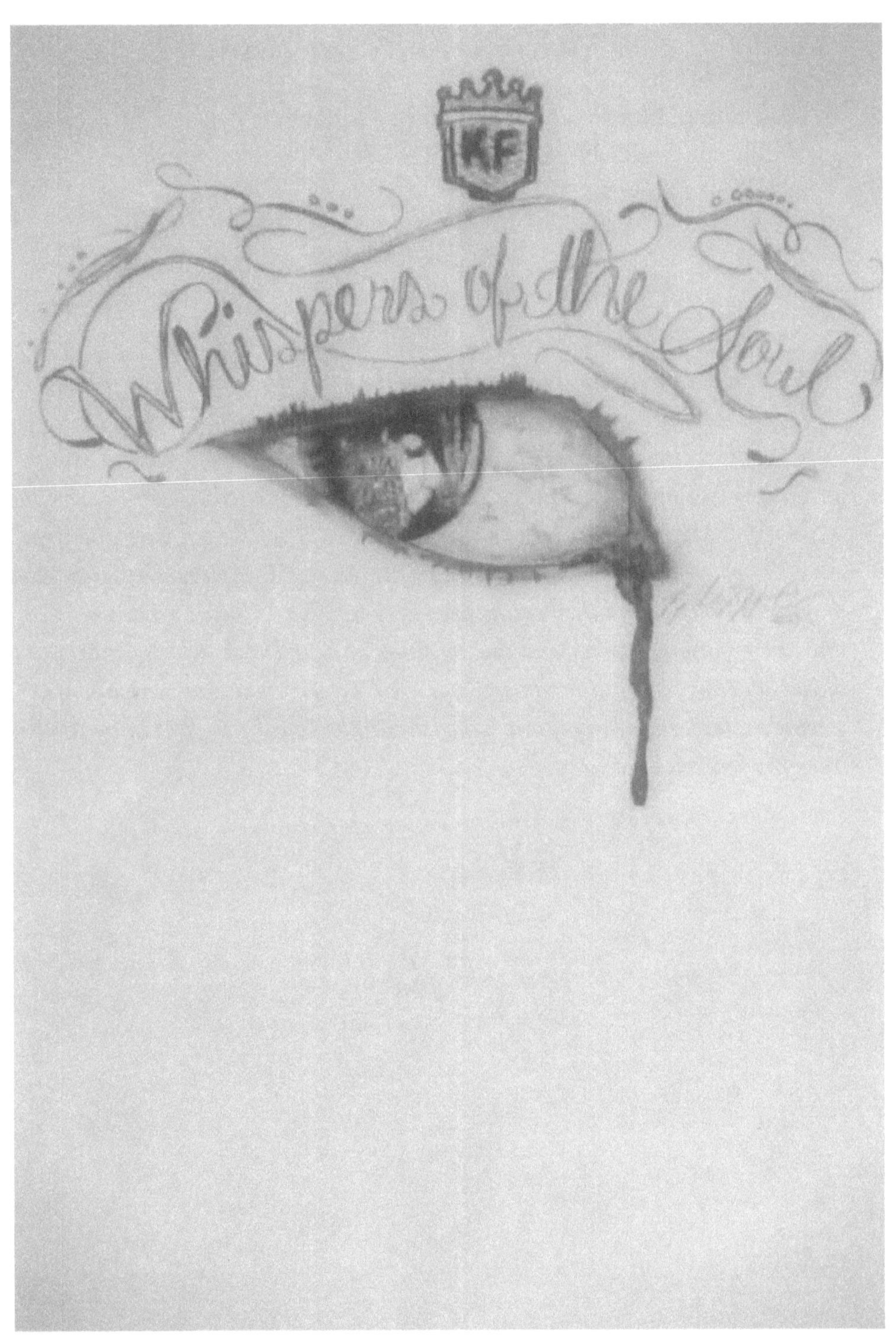

KF
Whispers of the Soul

Whispers of the Soul

Age rating: Not for children under 13
Publisher: SARAH ELLISONFLAKE
Category: Poetry

Whispers of the Soul is my battle in the form of poems. Poems that Speak the Language of Love and loss and lessons learned along the way. From heartbreak to love, demons to hell, all while dealing with mental health and ultimately finding solace and growth, these poems reflect the depths of the human experience. With empathy as the guiding force. I will delve into the pain and anguish of heartbreak. Through heartfelt verses, I explore shattered dreams, fragments of love, and the healing process that follows. These poems aim to capture the raw emotions experienced during times of heartbreak, offering solace to those who have endured similar trials. I hope these words resonate with your journey and provide solace, inspiration, and understanding. Thank you for taking the time to read my first book.

Chapter 1: My Story

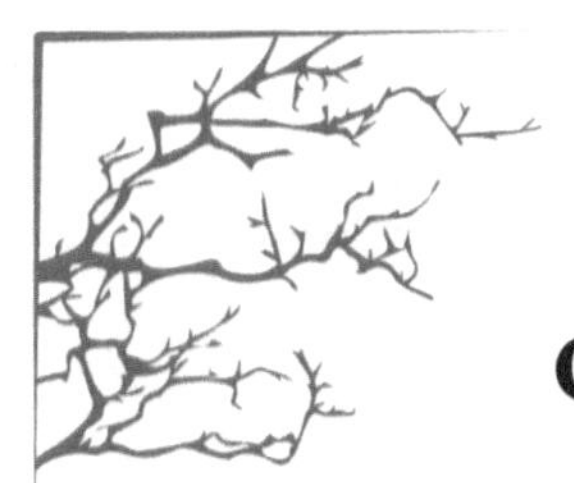

BELIEVE ME WHEN I SAY I know how it feels to be lost, struggling, and not know when my next meal might come, or where I can lay my head at.

That feeling of being so down and out that I needed the most basic things that most take for granted like food, a bed, and clean clothes. I decided instead of talking about helping others, I would be the one who started the helping, hoping to give back.

And one day, I will finally find my way out of this darkness.

I'm discovering how to start loving and I'm starting to figure things out slowly but surely. It ain't fast and it sure ain't been easy. Still, I'm thankful for my hell, and all the bad stuff that happened forged my strength so that I could fight the fires of my life.

All these things are what drive me to never give up, never stay down, and most importantly, never settle for less than what I deserve.

Let me tell you, it would have been so much easier to just quit but that's not who I am or will ever be. I have dreams, goals, and desires that I promised myself to always go after.

So that's what I'm doing,

relentlessly, tirelessly, and bravely. I hope! There's been a lot of hard days and I keep fucking up, but I know that this life is a journey, not just a fucking race.

My dreams don't have an expiration. I still have time.

As long as I believe in myself and know that there's nothing I can't or won't get through, I'll be okay.

So, I'm still taking it one day at a time. There'll be a day when I finally reach that place where I worked so hard to be and that's when I'll stop, take a deep breath, and breathe it all in just for a moment. Then, I'll turn around and find someone who is where I once was, just struggling,

trying to make their way.

I'll reach out my hand and help them.

together, we can rise.

That's my promise to myself. It's a promise that I fully intend to keep. It's something we can all do for one another.

This is my story!

Maybe it can be yours too!

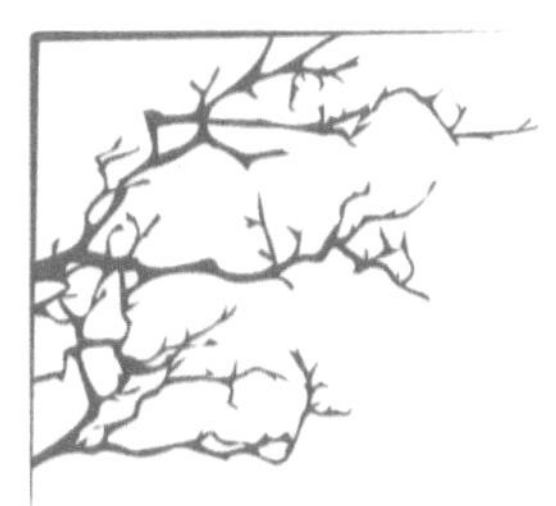

Chapter 2: Time??

I GOT A BOTTLE OF JACK, and a bottle of pills,
   and an Old 45 sitting here next to all these bills.
   It's all stacking up, and I feel so low,
   about to hit the point that I just let go.
   I stare at the mirror, and I shake my head,
   fighting back this feeling that I'm better off dead.
   Just why am I trying so hard anyway?
   I'm barely getting by.
   Always seems like I'm going through a war.
   I should have died a hundred times,
   no more like a thousand.
   Feeling guilty about all the mistakes that I've made.
   But the story is always pretty much the same,
   there never seems to be any change.
   I feel like I'm looking at the same old page.
   I'm stuck in this rut and seems there's no escape.
   I'm starting to believe that this is my fate.
   I'm staring at these bottles,
   and this loaded gun with tears in my eyes,
   black eyeliner running down my lips.
   I feel so fucking dumb.
   How did I get here? On the very edge, after all I lived through.
   All I've escaped?
   Sitting here contemplating if I'm ready to swallow these fuckin meds.
   There's no good answer, there's no way out.
   I've lost all respect for my stupid self.
   But as I sit here, I hear a sigh,
   a voice in my head telling me perhaps it's time.

Time? Time?
TIME!

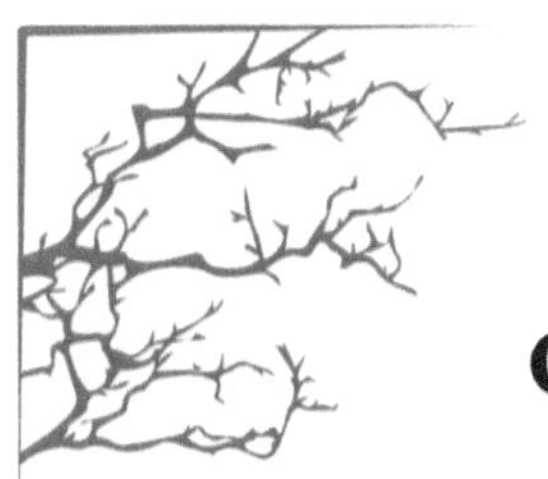

Chapter 3: All Alone

I CARRY TOO MUCH CRAZY for anyone to love. Made entirely of broken pieces. I'm no porcelain doll.

My mind is like a whirlwind, a tornado full of chaos and I keep getting cut on the glass from my past. My heart is hollowed, it's empty, but I still bleed.

But they've about bled this bitch dry, yet my heart still beats, no sympathy for the soul. I won't cry, despite these scars I carry. This pain. I wish it on no one, so I take it everywhere.

All Alone!!

Chapter 4: Work to do

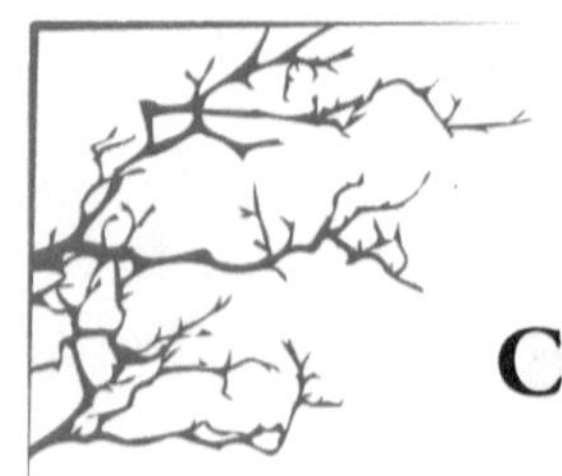

I WISH I COULD MAKE the silence just be quiet. It's anything but as I sit in the midst of this mess that I call my life.

All the things I should have done, all the promises I made, and all the hurt that I caused. All I can do in these moments is to remember and never open that door again.

Shut the door to the pain, the hurt, and the suffering. Never look back at the person that I was and try to embrace the person that I'm trying to become.

It's probably the hardest thing I've ever done, as it should be. It should burn and it should remind me every day of the bad choices that led me here.

For the first time in maybe forever, I know what it means to hope, to love, and to believe.

Yes, I know the road ahead is long and it will hurt every step that I take. But it needs to.

I don't want to ever return to that place where the darkness knows me by name, and I linger in all the pain. Mine, theirs, all.

Nothing worth having comes easy and I'm willing to pay that price. I am tired of the what if's and the could have beens.

I'm not going to tell you that I know the way, because I don't. Don't even have a freaking clue of where to find the path that leads me there.

But what I do know is this.

There will be a day, someday in the future, when I will lift my eyes to the mirror and realize for the first time in my life that I'm enough. When I can finally say I'm becoming the woman I should have been so very long ago.

I hope to see you down that road. But for now, I gotta go. I've got work to do.

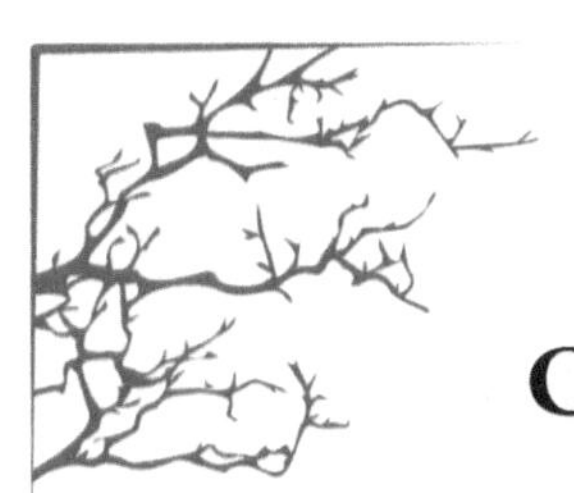

Chapter 5: Tick Tock

AND WHEN I THINK I'VE finally
found the right one,
I realize how wrong I am.
And when the conversation
gets deep, then deeper,
I think I lose my mind completely,
until I forget
what I'm looking for in reality.
Sometimes I forget who I am
trying to be the person my person
needs by their side.
And when I think I'm going to be fine,
something bad always happens.
But I refuse to give in or give up,
that's when the pain cuts me
until the tears fall down.
Until I fall down.

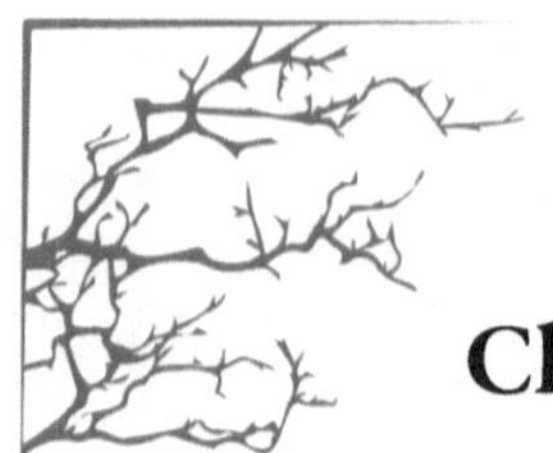

Chapter 6: Drained and Empty

I DESPISE THESE SLEEPLESS nights when sleep just seems to escape me, and my restless mind relentlessly convinces me of all my flaws and all my failures. My troubled thoughts, scream that freedom is just out of reach. I feel trapped in a body that seems to turn on me, wanting to destroy me. I hate these nights when I feel I'm not living up to my full potential, feeling isolated, and lacking the toughness that others possess. As I lie here, gazing at the ceiling, searching for answers in the chipped paint above me. I've learned to escape the confines of my existence and instead search through the rooms in my dreams. These nights bring a wave of animosity, making me believe that everything, even my very soul, is drained and empty of all energy.

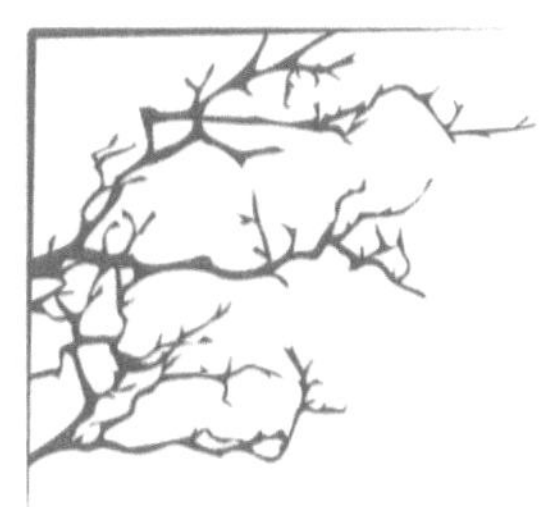

Chapter 7: Talk

WHEN "I LOVE YOU" TURNS to hate,
and there's nothing left to save,
when you're surrounded by
all the memories, ghosts, and graves,
I think that's the moment when you find out what's
deep inside your soul.
If you're nothing but a graveyard,
or if you let it lay you low.
Some might call you chickenshit.
for holding back your truth.
When it's in ruins all around you,
And you don't have any glue
to put it back together even if the was a "together" to be found again.
When "I love you" lay in shambles,
in scattered, broken pieces all over the ground,
just leave them to their small minds and unwanted opinions.
It doesn't matter what they say,
it's not their heart that's broken,
it's not their dreams inside that coffin locked inside that grave.
Their ghost can never haunt you,
they're just voices on the wind
with no fucking clue what sustains you.
What made you live again,
when it all came down to nothing?
You found the strength to get up and walk,
so let them call you what they will,
cause that's all they've got,
and that's just simple-minded talk.

Chapter 8: Battle I Face

I'M FIGHTIN' DEMONS, some days it's a struggle to just hold on.
I'm broken, drugs the fault, but this war ain't over let me tell you son.
In the depths of my mind, darkness takes its toll.
But I'm a rise from this hell, gonna claim back my soul.

Cursing and hurting,
    this pain is my fuel.
Gonna show these demons that they just fools.
So I'll spit my fire and ignite, unleash with all my might.

Fightin' back,
    I'm a warrior in the night.
Unseen battles,
demons put up a fight.
But I'm coming up,
I ain't backing down.
Scratch the surface,
I'll make them drown.

Demon's whispers echoing
        in my mind,
but I'm stopping these thoughts,
I'll leave them far behind.
Seeking redemption in this world,
the unforgiving shuffle.
I won't let them win, no,
I won't buckle.

So many nights,
        I've fought this fight alone.
But I won't surrender,
I'll turn these demons to stone.
There's power in my voice,
my rage, it won't go unheard.
With every verse I write,
their fate is sealed, it's absurd.
They tell me I'm weak,
that I'll never stand tall.
But they can't see the strength in my battle call.
Saying fuck you to the doubters.
I rise from the ground.
With every punch I swing, their hope is drowned.

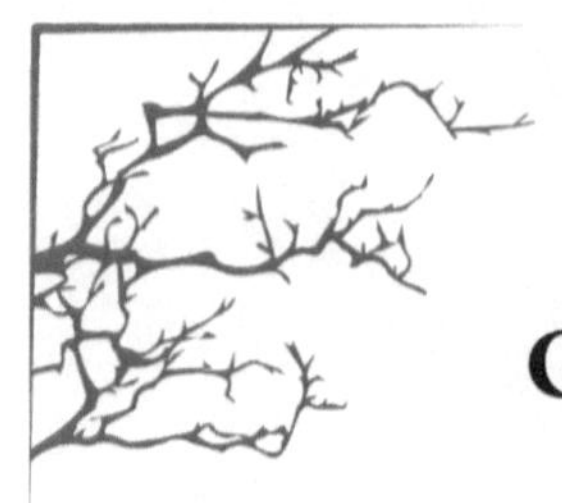

Chapter 9: Burn it all

IMA HAVE MYSELF A BONFIRE
    with everything you ever gave me.
    Throw some magick on the flames,
    and maybe that might save me.
    Ima burn it all to nothing,
    till only ash remains.
    I'll take that ash and make some ink.
    and write my own chapter.
    I'll move into the future,
    I'll leave you in my past.
    You can already see the steps I've been taking.
    You can kiss my ass,
    I'm done with all we ever were.
    Throw some magick on the flames!
    You'd best hope someone catches you,
    that's one long-assed way to fall.
    I've held you up for far too long.
    It's time I show the truth,
    I'm done with being stupid,
    and I've got no use for fools.
    My only wish for you is karma,
    "May you get just what you've given."
    I've shouted love for far too long,
    and every word I've written,
    yep, Ima have myself a bonfire
    with every page I ever wrote.
    When the flames die down to nothing,
    You'll just be another ghost

with no power left to haunt me with.
No regret left in my soul,
Ima have myself a bonfire
and I'll finally be whole.
The pieces that you took from me,
It's time I got them all back.
I wish you nothing but the best,
But it's way too fucking late for that.

Chapter 10: Waiting for the Next Chapter!

"DARKNESS, IT'S BEEN a while, but you never really left, did you?"
Here I was once more face to face with the darkness
that seemed to periodically rear its fucking ugly head.
I had always done whatever I had to make it go away,
to stop it from haunting all my waking thoughts.
But the truth is, it was always going to be there
until I learned to confront it.
Until I stop running and stop lying to myself
because everything is not okay.
I always end up back here.
I let the fear almost take me,
I thought I ran far enough where I was past it.
I never was.
That's the thing about darkness and personal demons,
they just don't disappear on their own.
You are the only way they will ever be gone from your life.
I don't know why I never understood why
I thought I could outsmart their darkness.
Once more, I stood at a crossroads in my life.
Waiting for the next chapter.
A younger me would have done anything to hide,
bury the truth so deeply that it couldn't hurt me anymore.
But that's not the way it works.
I could either banish it or keep doing what I had always done,
which had never truly worked.
I was tired.
I was tired of running.

WHISPERS OF THE SOUL

I was tired of lying to myself.
I was tired of being afraid.
This time, that crossroad in my life felt just a little bit different.
It was still all the things that chilled me to my bones,
but now there was something more.
And then, I understood.
I began to believe, to realize that I was enough.
I started to believe that I could break the cycle.
It's amazing what the smallest amount of hope will do.
It can literally change your life.
Yes, I was faced with the darkness that had plagued me my entire life.
Only now, I had stopped running.
I did what I never could have imagined before,
I embraced the darkness.
Then and only then did I see the light seeping
through the darkness of my soul.
I'm done running.
Bring it on darkness,
I'm ready.
It's time for me to find the light.

Chapter 11: Sleep, What's that?

IF THERE'S NO REST for the wicked,
    then I must be the worst.
    Because I wouldn't know rest
    If it was introduced first.
    Actual sleep is a neighbor
    who very rarely drops by.
    Peaceful dreams are just strangers,
    not known to my eyes.
    I don't sleep that often,
    and never in peace,
    I wake up still crying
    from heartbroken dreams.
    Don't know 'bout the wicked"
    but there's no rest for me.
    Hasn't been in some time,
    and it seems now it never will be.

Chapter 12: Strength to Overcome

WHO IS THIS PERSON I have let myself become?
To the world around me, I'm so numb.
A slave to these drugs, I will always succumb.
It's hard to believe I used to think of this as fun.
With this life, I am almost done.
I've lost myself in this dark and endless run,
In search of something that can't be won.
These pills and potions have taken their toll,
Leaving behind an empty soul.
Once vibrant and alive, now a mere shadow,
Yearning for the days when my heart would glow.
The highs were temporary, but the lows remain,
A constant reminder of my self-inflicted pain.
I long for the clarity that sobriety would bring,
To break free from these chains and start anew again.
But addiction holds me tightly in its grip,
Whispering lies that make it hard to resist.
I'm drowning in a sea of regret and shame,
Wondering if anyone will remember my name.
This battle within me rages on each day,
I question if there's still a chance for change.
But deep down, I know there's hope yet to come,
If only someone could help me find the strength to overcome.

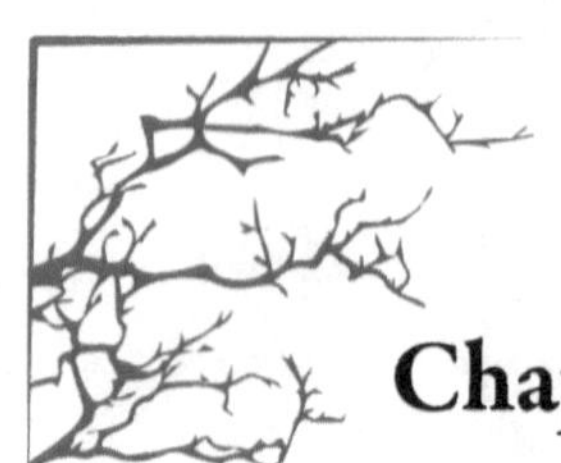

Chapter 13: The Long Road

RUNNING FROM GOD, I was lost in the dark
   Chasing after dreams but it tore me apart.
   Thought I could find peace in a different path,
   but it led me to pain, nothing but wrath.
   Fueled by the drugs, trying to escape reality,
   but it only brought chaos, a twisted mentality.

But I realized that running ain't the way to survive.
   Gotta face the truth, and keep the drive alive.
No more turning back, it's time to make a change.
Break free from these chains, break free from this pain.

Gave up on my dreams and thought I couldn't achieve them.
   But deep inside, I knew I had to believe.
Lost my twins because I wasn't there for 'em.
So, now I'm biting down on this leather, gotta hold on,
gotta do what God said He made me for.

Biting down while growling.

OMG, NO more numbing the pain?
But no more sinking in despair!
Gotta take control, gotta show that I care.
I'm fighting for a better life, break these chains.
Show them what I'm made of.
Even though a lil insane,
I'mma prove to my babies that their mother remains.

But I'm realizing that running ain't the way to survive.
Gotta face the truth, gotta keep my drive alive.
No more turning back, it's time I made a change.
Break free from these chains, break free from this pain.

Now I'm on this mission, gotta make amends.
Mending broken bridges gotta make new friends.
No more running, I'm facing my fears.
Taking responsibility as I wipe away the tears.

My twins, forgive me, please.
This road I'm on is long and really hard,
Be patient!
No more drugs, no more running away.
Gotta be a beacon in the night and show the way.
I'ma be the mother you deserve every single day

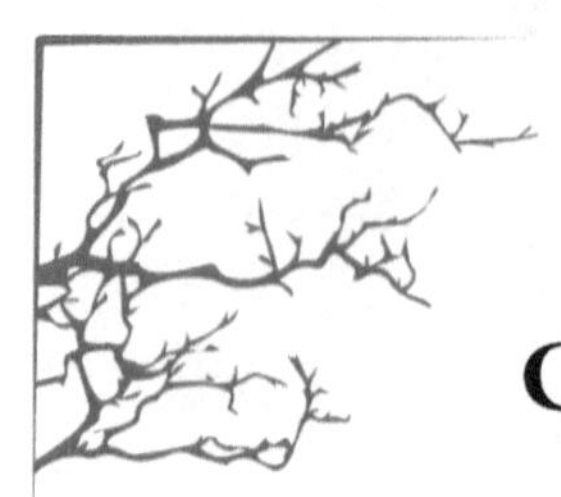

Chapter 14: Seriously

DEPRESSION IS NOT JUST the blues.
Anxiety is more than just a lil worrying.
P.T.S.D. is not just thinking about the past.
Bipolar is so much more than mood swings.
There is no one-size-fits-all treatment.
There is no wishing it all away.
Many mental health issues are sadly here to stay.
BREAK the CYCLE.
STOP the STIGMA.

Chapter 15: Center stage

THERE WAS NOTHING LEFT before her,
or of the dreams she'd left behind.
Just an open road of sorrow,
and the music in her head.
Melodies of memories.
A soundtrack of the past,
eating up the miles
with a foot made for fast.
As if no one could ever catch her.
She might just outrun the demons
those memories made,
where love and hope are on center stage.
Those demons had it made,
they simply had to shine so bright
and then abruptly fade.
That's all it takes to kill a soul,
whose only dream was love.
When that was all they tried to be,
but they never were enough.
She tries to push those thoughts aside
and sees the cliff ahead.
She races for that Finish Line.
There's no memories when you're dead.

Chapter 16: Happily, Ever After

GETTING LOST WITHIN my mind,
It's not a healthy place to be.
So many dark & twisted thoughts,
that mock reality.
Most of them are memories
I will never escape.
Some are fucking landmines,
they wanna see me break.
How much can I take? I wonder
before I'm really lost for good?
And I wonder when I'm gone will anybody
know I fought as hard as I could?
Or will they think I just gave up?
Does it even really matter?
I think that
some of us were never meant
for happily-ever-after.

Chapter 17: I Know How to Disappear

I KNOW WHERE I'M GOING,
    I know it isn't here.
    I know how to just get gone,
    to simply disappear.
    It's time for me to move on.
    I'm running out of time.
    The hourglass is going empty,
    and the words are out of rhyme.
    There's nothing here that's left for me,
    just some ghosts from days long past.
    I wonder if they'll go with me
    when I leave this place at last.
    Just more shit that doesn't matter, much,
    except within my mind.
    It's hell to act like I don't care,
    when I'm really not like that.
    It's past time I move on,
    I've done all I can.
    I'll leave behind the memories,
    and let my heartache take the stand.
    No comment, sir, next question.
    Yes, It's the only thing I've ever known.
    Even if it wasn't real,
    just dreams that someone made up for me,
    it was still everything.
    So, I'll take it all when I go.

Chapter 18: Finish Line

THERE WAS NOTHING LEFT before her,
of the dreams she'd left behind.
Just this open road of sorrow,
and the music in her head.
Melodies of memories,
a soundtrack of the past,
eating up the miles,
with a foot made of lead to be fast,
it's as though if she kept driving
at a speed no one could catch her,
fingers crossed,
she might just outrun her demons.
Those memories surely hatched,
where Love and Hope were center stage.
Those demons had it made,
they simply had to shine brightly,
and then abruptly fade.
That's all it takes to kill a soul
whose only dream was love.
When that was all they tried to be,
but they never were enough.
She tries hard to push those thoughts aside.
Then she sees the cliff ahead.
She races for that Finish Line.
There are no more memories when you're dead.

Chapter 19: Darkness My Angel's Standing There

IN THE DEPTHS OF MY darkness, lost in this despair,

Drugs took hold of me, my soul, that demon stripped bare.

They whispered promises, but illusions are what they spun.

Little did I know, my life was already coming undone.

Luring me in with promises of temporary bliss.

Instead, I found myself trapped in an endless abyss.

Drugs took me for one hell of a ride, consuming my very being.

But during the chaos, I had angels standing nearby,

They felt the pain and saw the struggle I faced,

and with compassion, they never hesitated to caress. No judgment,

not a trace.

They spoke to me gently; their voice was a guiding light.

Reminding me of the strength within, so lit.

They gave me hope, it was a lifeline for me to hold.

At that moment, I felt a flicker of my dream unfold.

Words spoken were a comfort, a reason to believe, yes to

believe that I could overcome this darkness and find the real me

that was buried deep within myself.

I found the strength to try.

Started fighting the demons within, to LIVE and not just survive.

So, if you ever face this despair, remember this tale,

that even in darkness, there's always a path.

Reach out to a friend, a lifeline, their words of comfort will help

you stay and fight.

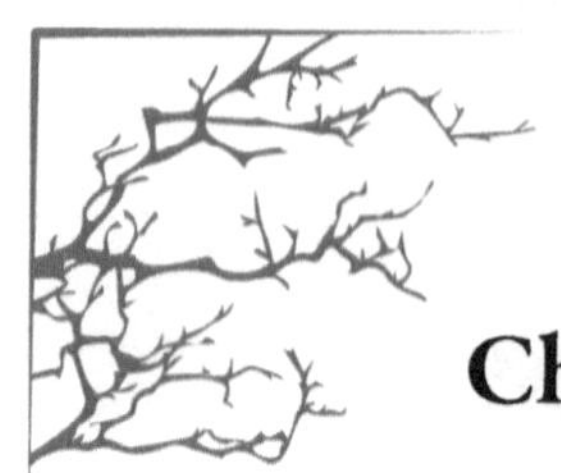

Chapter 20: Battle Scars

I BOTTLE PAIN LIKE I breathe air,
  without a second thought
  and I'll never let them see me cry especially,
  if they're the ones at fault.
  This has been my lifetime mantra
  for as long as I recall.
  And I might bleed when I hit bottom,
  but won't ever tell who made me fall.
  If you're close enough to hurt me,
  if I've let you in that far
  then I can only blame myself
  for my soul's newest battle scars.

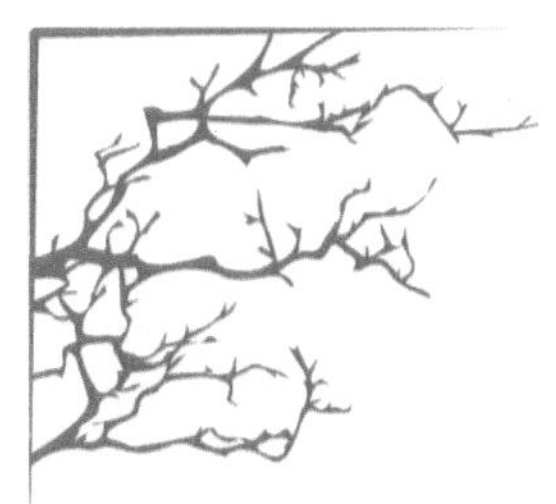

Chapter 21: Karma

MAKING DECISIONS YOU can't come back from,
on a night when nobody even fuckin cares.
Staring at the darkness just
to find there's nobody there.
Takes a strength that few are even aware of or made of.
In this world of broken promises and hidden cries,
where everything is nothing,
and every "TRUTH" is just more fuckin "LIES".
There's escaping and then there's running.
Sometimes they aren't the same.
When the bottom keeps rising, won't stop it just keeps coming,
and it seems even love is a fuckin game they all seem to play.
Just watch me,
I'll show you what I'm made of.
I told you once before,
"When my words are made of nothing but silence,
you'll understand the war
you chose to fight".
I've decided and guess what,
I didn't even fuckin cry.
You're nothing now but pieces
of a lost and broken past.
You might think you've won,
but you can bet your last dollar that I'll be standing last.
Your karma will keep coming,
cause of the decisions you made, and the heart's you broke with no
remorse.
Based on you're lying heart,

where love is just a figment
that could never even fucking exist.
I've decided
you're not one I'll miss.
I hope you learn from all this at least before you take your last
breath.
The path you chose is one of a rocky ending,
and no one will escape the wrath
of karma in the end.
She'll settle all her scores.
She'll show you less is never more.
So, see ya,
I'm on my way to better things,
while your destiny is to be lost
in a ocean of nobody fuckin cares.
You'll pay the final cost
you tried to lay on me.
Trust me, karma knows the difference, and baby you, I guarantee
she'll serve with a smile upon her lips.

Chapter 22: Unbreakable Bond

I SEE YOUR PAIN, AND like Chucky, I'll be your friend till the end.

In this world full of madness, I understand your pain.

Facing battles all alone, that's no way to live life, I know.

I feel your pain, can't you see?

Together we can conquer anything, you and me.

I'm here, I love you, don't you ever give up, it's not in our DNA. We are not wired that way.

You're amazing, and strong, and you got that tough stuff in you.

In this cold world, it's hard to find a real one.

But just know I got your back, no matter what you go through,

Fighting demons, facing endless battles on your own,

Bet, I'm right here, I feel your pain, can't you see?

Life throws curveballs, trust me, I know it well.

Resilience is key, and that's what you gotta pursue.

Sometimes life ain't fair, it's a treacherous game that I know all too well.

But we won't back down, we can't, no, we'll never be tame.

In unity we find strength, that's the truth. I feel your pain, can't you see?

So, let's face this world, head held high.

A bond unbreakable, even beyond the sky. Remember,

You're not alone,

Keep fighting, keep shining.

I love you.

Take my hand.

Chapter 23: Strength is a default

STRENGTH HAS BEEN MY default
for as long as I recall.
It's how I've survived everything
from the time that I was small.
Walls made of titanium.
Wired with C-4.
So, all that wants to kill me
can't make it through the door.
At least that's what it looks like.
but the reality is it's just a shell,
it's everything I hide behind
when life goes straight to hell.
This time it's like cardboard
that's been left out in the rain.
Just one touch would break it,
it can't withstand anymore.
Each raindrop makes it weaker
than the one that fell before.
The storm is getting stronger
and it can't take much more.
I don't know if I'll make it through,
I think I've lost too much.
My mind is full of yesterday.
My heart's been ground to dust.
Strength might be my default,
but somebody's hit reset,
cuz now I'm falling faster

through this darkness without a fucking net.
I'm writing this to remind you,
check on even your strongest friends,
cuz sometimes strength is cardboard
that can't hold up in the end.

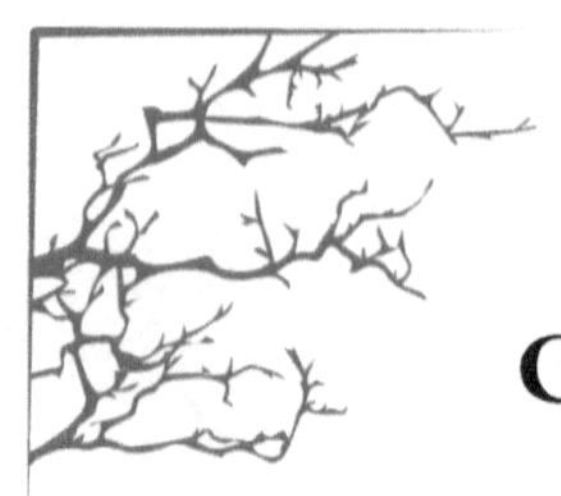

Chapter 24: Monsters

POUNDING ON EACH DOOR you pass
Screaming down the hall
Blood flowing like a river
You slip, you slide, you fall.
You glance behind you quickly
at the monsters getting closer with each breath.
Evil voices fill the air,
screaming, twisted ghosts.
You know if they catch you
you'll die screaming; you'll die slow.
You know they'll drain you dry, again,
then try to steal your soul.
Your heart is pounding loudly,
nearly drowning out the sounds
of bloody, soulless terror
that, EVERYWHERE, still abounds.,
Now you're running blindly
as the evil ghosts give chase.
There has to be an exit
out of this Hell-bound place.
Flying 'round the corner
you spot way up ahead
a square of blessed hope,
yet your soul is filled with dread.
You know you'll never make it,
it's too far down the hall.
Then bony fingers snatch at your hair
and you begin to fall

into a light so blinding
no darkness can exist,
and you realize that your running
would always end like this.,
A period to a sentence.
A stone upon a grave.
But at least you went down swinging
with every step you ever made,
and you know that counts for something
now that it's finally done.
You gave your all and faltered,
yet, somehow, you still won.

Chapter 25: Living for the Night

SHE LIVED FOR THE NIGHT wrapped around herself,
hidden away from their prying eyes.
Time to come undone.
No more disguises.
Tears fall silently,
dripping to the floor.
Here, in solitude where she can take no more.
Breathe in.
Breathe out.
Getting no air.
Wrapped in the darkness where safety is a lie.
Hidden away.
Barely getting by.

Chapter 26: Mental health awareness

I DON'T JUMP BECAUSE something MIGHT happen, I jump because it already has.

I don't sleep a lot because the darkness becomes too hard to fight. I'm constantly exhausted, and constantly on edge.

This is who I am, now. I have C-PTSD, Bipolar, and Severe Depression. This is who I am, and who I'll always be.

This is how life strangles me.

Chapter 27: One without the other

YOU CAN'T HAVE ONE without the other.
They both go hand in hand.
And if you don't get that now
well, you'll never understand.
Darkness is the backdrop.
The sun needs it to shine,
while the moon holds all the diamonds
and pulls at all the tides.
And people think they're balanced
when they're shouting "love & light"
refusing to acknowledge
they can't survive without the night.
Until we got to where we are
humanity just lost.
For they all went their separate ways
and now we all pay the cost.

Chapter 28: Happy ending

HOW DID SO MUCH COME to nothing?
Leaving just an empty space
when everything was over,
and there were no truths left to face
except for this aching wall of silence
with a window to the past that
highlights where it all went wrong
and where we tried to make it last.
It's almost like a crime scene, now.
Missing just the chalked-up outline
to represent the bodies
who we were there before the fault line
came crashing down around us
like a plane, we couldn't fly
or an ocean bent on flooding
every dream that was held inside.
I look around that empty room
deep inside my soul
to remind myself of all I've lost and that
there's nothing left in there for me.
It's time to lock the door
and leave behind the memories
of who I was before.
That one brief shining moment.
Those too few years.
That was only a fairytale,
there's no happy ending, there.

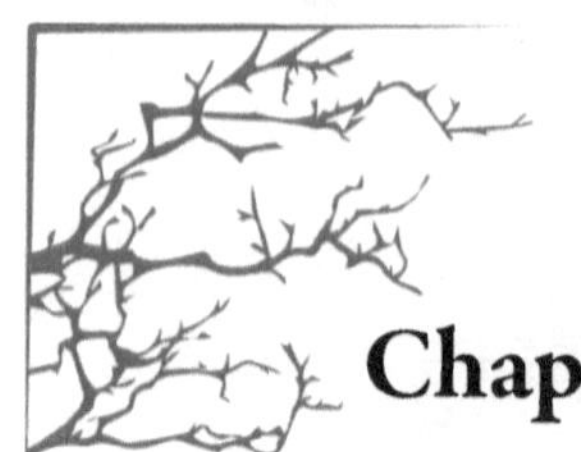

Chapter 29: Not a 'Z' in sight

7:30 IN THE MORNING
    not a "Z" in sight.
    I've been staring at the ceiling
    this entire fucking night.
    Shadows fade on the walls
    as the dawn moves in.
    Like the night is somewhere
    sleep never should've been.
    And the tired grows.
    And the tired grows.
    The tired grows!
    And the sleepless strikes!
    Another hope grows cold
    that I'll get sleep tonight.
    As the sun comes up
    the night just goes.
    Throughout my body
    the tired grows,
    the tired grows.

Chapter 30: Letter She'll Never Read

MY DEAR DAUGHTER,

As I sit here, writing this letter to you, tears stream down my face, and my heart aches with regret. I want you to know how deeply I love you and how sorry I am for allowing drugs to take over my life. It is a burden I have carried for way too long, and it is time for me to face the consequences of my actions.

Once upon a time, our lives were filled with joy and laughter. You were my little princess sugar britches. We would spend hours playing in the park. But somewhere along the way, I lost sight of what truly mattered.

The darkness of addiction slowly crept into my life, clouding my judgment. I was no longer the mama you deserved, but a mere shell of the woman I once was.

I heard the disappointment in your voice every time I promised to change, only to break that promise once again. Drowning in my own despair, unable to break free from these chains that held me captive.

Drugs led me down a
path filled with pain, loneliness, and despair. I lost everything that mattered to me – you and your brother, my friends, but worst of all, your trust. I've become a stranger to my children, a ghost haunting the hallways, unable to connect with the world around me.

Kiaya, darling, please know that through this dark journey, my love for you never wavered. It burned like a flickering candle, fighting against the winds of addiction, desperately trying to stay alive. I may have failed you as a mom, but my love for you remained constant, even in the depths of my hell.

I want to be the mom you deserve, the one who will always love you unconditionally.

I know that words alone cannot erase the pain and heartache I have caused you, but I hope that someday you will find it in your heart to forgive me. Kiaya, please remember that you are not defined by my mistakes. You are a beautiful, strong, and resilient young lady with a world of opportunities just ahead. Do not let my past define your future. Learn from my mistakes and let them be a reminder of the strength and courage that lies within you. I love you more than words can express, and I am eternally sorry for the pain I have caused.

With all my love,

Your mom

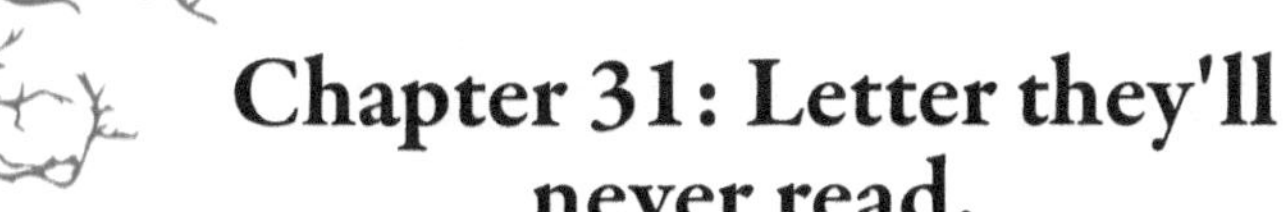

Chapter 31: Letter they'll never read.

I APOLOGIZE TO MY KIAYA and my Kris, my babies, my twins, for leaving them behind, lost in my sins, drugs took over, clouding my mind and my soul. But now I'm here just trying to make things whole.

I pray you never truly understand what I mean when I say, I let the darkness consume me, lost in its grip. Oh, but now I see the damage caused by this horrible trip.

Kiaya and Kris, forgive me for the pain I've caused, I'll fight this battle, no matter the cost. The road to redemption won't be easy or fast, but I'll make it right, somehow, since I'm no longer living in the past. Kiaya and Kris, no more promises, I'm gonna show you, I got to. and pray that we can heal and be a family,

Chapter 32: Never Mattered

I THOUGHT I KNEW ITS taste,
I'd tasted it, before,
but never here in Wonderland,
where every less is even more.
I knew it was a bad idea,
one that I'd regret.
Still, I did it, anyway
for no drug has killed me yet.
And, damn, did it feel good, at first.
Like no ride ever before.
I smoked it like I was losing a race.
It filled me with euphoria,
it killed me like a deadly sin.
Slowly bleeding out my heart
each time I drew the smoke in.
Then suddenly it turned to acid,
eating me alive.
As I swallowed the betrayal,
I didn't know if I'd survive.
That pain that filled my body.
The way that my soul shattered
when I swallowed down th truth,
"That I never even Fucking mattered".

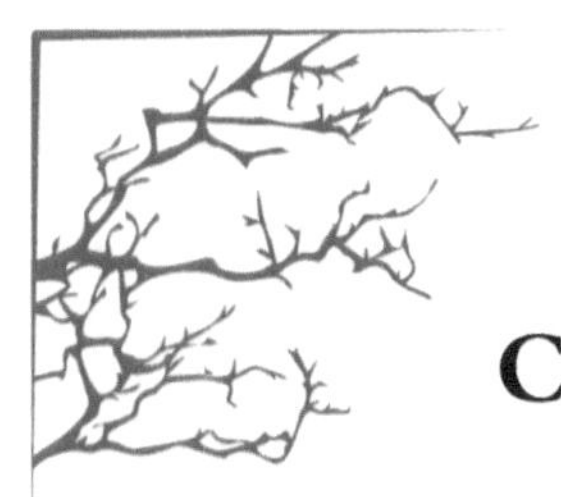

Chapter 33: Bad Again

I KNOW IT'S GETTING bad again
    when I don't want to be here, I don't wanna live this life of mine.
    And all the things that could've been
    are saying, baby, just disappear, bye, bye, bye.
    Like a ghost trapped in the night
    that nobody can see,
    dying for a little light
    in all this misery.
    I think of all that I've survived and
    it makes me wonder why.
    Why I struggle just to stay alive
    when really, I just want to die.
    Finally, leave this wretched earth
    that has no place for me.
    Since the first day of my birth
    there's been no place for me to be.
    But my soul was made to fight,
    war is all I've got left to give.
    Someday, perhaps I'll get it right
    and find a way to live
    at peace with all I battle inside
    and everyone I lost.
    Until then I'll fight this wave of depression,
    I've already paid the cost time and time again,
    so, there's no point in giving in or giving up.
    The price paid was much too fucking dear.
    I hear God whisper, "Stop,
    you're still needed, here."

He tells me the road I'm walking
is one only I can walk,
that I was sent to write, and I can't do that dead.
But as I write these words
things they just don't seem real.
I've been blessed, and I've been cursed
with all I fucking feel.

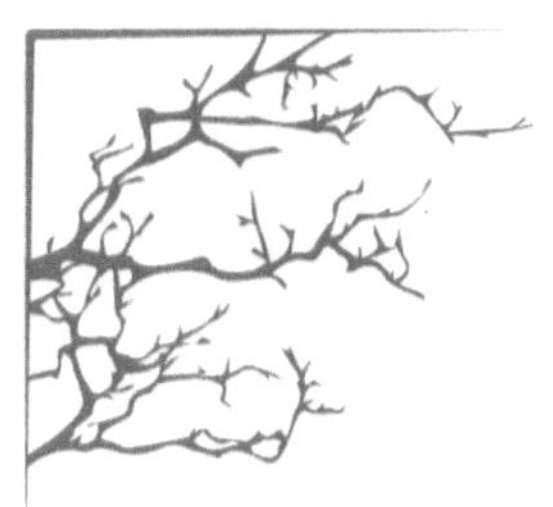

Chapter 34: Theif

THE VEIL IS GROWING thinner,
    but the weight will never cease.
    Some days a breath of oxygen
    just brings me to my knees.
    It wasn't supposed to be this way,
    that's a thought I have too much
    for someone in the land of life
    with only death to touch.
    One by one, I lost them
    and with each one, I died.
    Some days there's nothing left of me
    except for the tears I've cried,
    oceans made of memories,
    waterfalls of pain,
    rivers full of yesterday,
    storms of silent rain.
    They say that time heals everything,
    but there's no healing grief.
    Truth is time's criminal,
    cuz it's just a fucking thief.

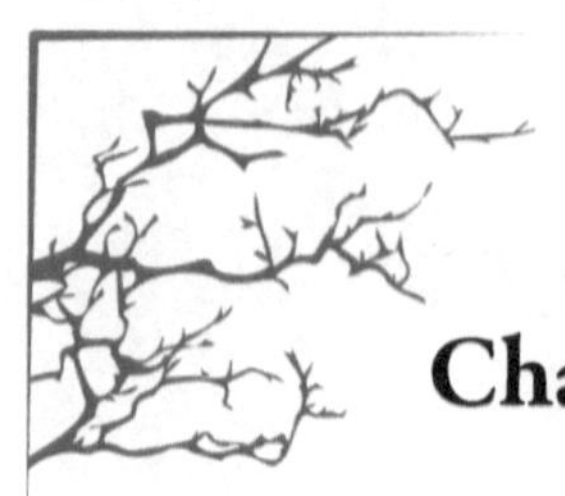# **Chapter 35: Next Chapter**

IN YOUR EYES, LOVE'S flame ignites.
A symphony of emotions, my heart takes flight.
You are the sun that brightens my day,
the moon that guides me when darkness holds me in its sway.
I love you, with all of my being.
A love so deep, forever, I'm foreseeing.
You're the best thing that's ever happened, it's so very true.
A treasure, a blessing, forever in my view.
You bring laughter and joy to most every day.
You lift my spirits; you make me whole.
Here we go, the next chapter.
A love story written in our souls.
Through highs and lows, together we will stand.
Hand in hand, walking side by side.
With you by my side, life's journey is complete.
In your embrace, my heart finds its own beat.
So, remember this, my love,
you are cherished and adored in every single way.
I love you, endlessly,
For you are the best thing that's ever happened to me.

Chapter 36: Battle of the Unseen

I'M FIGHTING DEMONS, it's a struggle just to hold on.

I'm broken, drugs are the blame, but this war ain't over yet, the depths of my mind, darkness takes its toll.

But I'm a rise like no other, gonna claim, NO, take back my soul.

Cursing and hurting, this pain is my fuel.

Gotta show these demons they're just fools.

I'll cuss, spitfire, and ignite, unleash all my might.

Fightin' back, I'm a warrior in the night.

Unseen battles, demons put up a fight.

But still, I rise, I ain't backing down.

Scratch the surface, I'll make them drown.

Demon's whispers echo in my mind, but I'm stopping these thoughts, I'll leave them far behind.

Seeking redemption in this world, the unforgiving shuffle.

I won't let them win, no, I won't back down.

So many nights, I've fought this fight alone.

But I won't surrender, I'll turn them demons to stone.

There's power in my voice, my rage, it won't go unheard.

With every verse I write, their fate is sealed, absurd.

They tell me I'm weak, that I'll never stand tall.

But they don't see the strength in my battle yell.

Saying fuck you to the doubters, I rise from the ground.

With every punch I swing, their hope is drowned.

Profound.

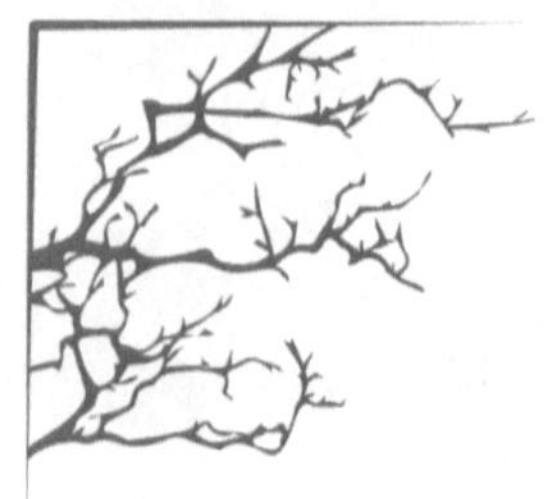

Chapter 37: Fight

IN THE DEPTHS OF MY darkness, where shadows hide,
a battle ensues, and demons collide.
Within the chaos, a whisper takes hold,
A voice of despair, with a story ready to be told.
It whispers you're
life is nothing, you're a failure, it cries.
Words so heavy, that all hope slowly dies.
But amid the mind torment, a flicker, a light,
an angel steps forward, ready to fight.
With wings of grace, and a heart and soul filled with love,
The angel whispers gently,
Your story ain't over yet, dear soul, redemption can be found.
The demon sneers, its anger unleashed,
trying to break free, to silence my newfound belief.
Yet the angel persists, its presence so profound,
Guiding my soul, to higher ground.
In this eternal struggle, both forces dance.
One pulling you down, the other one, so divine.
A truth starts unfolding,
that even in the darkness, our soul can't be sold.
For life is a journey, with valleys and paths,
The oldest tapestry is woven, with both joy and heartbreak.
I'm gonna stumble and fall to my knees, but I'm gonna keep
dragging myself back up and I know
my soul and spirit will endure, rise above it all.
So, fear not the battle between demons and angels,
for it is through struggle, we learn to live.
Embrace the fight, make it yours.

WHISPERS OF THE SOUL

Is your soul in the darkness? Honey have faith, do not give up, and i promise your
the soul will shine brightly again.

49

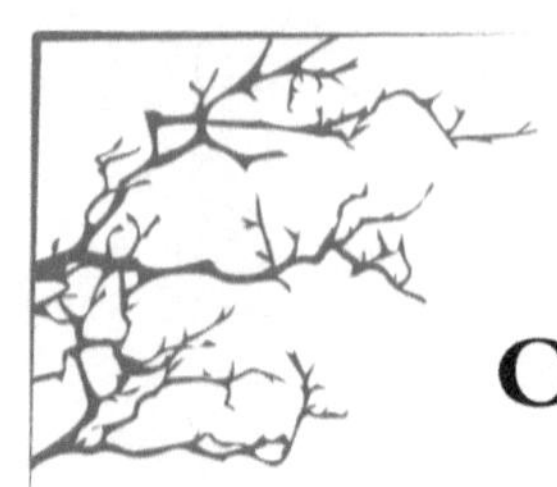

Chapter 38: Never Did

YOU DON'T KNOW ME.
You only know the words that I write.
Yes, I'm a soul that just bleeds,
but you don't know me.
You think that I'm the one
who'll turn blind eyes away
from the bullshit you're selling,
still trying to buy a new day,
but you don't know me.
I see you, now, you're
in technicolor bright.
Karma has a way
of bringing all things to its light.
You think because I'm dark that
I'm the villain in this sordid tale.
But what you fail to understand is,
I'm the balance in the scales.
So just know that I'm watching,
and know that now I see.
And yes, I know you thought you knew me,
but best believe,
you never really did.

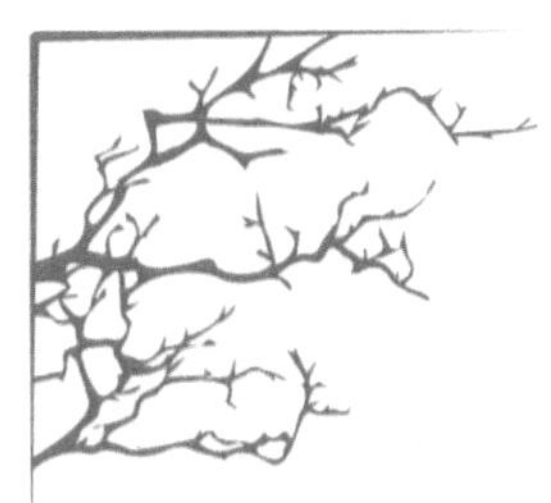

Chapter 39: Music

[VERSE 1]

I grew up in a big city, where dreams were even bigger, but hopes were small.

I got tangled up on a hell-bent path, thought I had it all under control.

But the devil kept whispering, he kept calling my name.

Led me down this road that has brought me nothing but pain.

[Chorus]

This is my battle, the fight that I face.

A story of redemption, finding strength in God's Grace.

Throughout all the highs and lows, I've learned to stand tall.

Thankful for everyone who's helped me heal, it's been one song at a time - y'all

[Verse]

In the smoke of broken promises, I lost myself along the way.
      Fell into the grip of spells and potions, searching for an escape.
But through the darkest nights, I found a thread of hope.
Music.
Yeah, Music, that soul-searching, truth-telling,
no holds barred, straight-from-the heart lyrics.
There were many of nights that Jelly Roll's music saved me from me,
for real ya'll

[Bridge]

Now I'm crawling out of the shadows, leaving my past behind.
      Scars will remind me, but they no longer define me.
With every chord and each lyric, a new chapter is being told.
The power of music made me find my soul.
[Outro]

So let this be a voice for those who fight their tormenting wars.
      There's a brighter side waiting, beyond the pain and closing doors.
With love and support, no mountain's too high.
Together we'll rise, leaving those old struggles far behind.

Chapter 40: Rolling Thru Life

I WAS BORN IN A BIG city
with dreams a lot bigger than that city.
I keep a pen in my hand,
and a journal by my side.
Just rolling through this life.
Makin' my dreams take flight.
Gonna write these words until they turn into poems,
cause I know it won't be long.
Yeah, I can do it, pave the way to a better life.
I've had my share of struggles,
but I won't let that hold me down.
With each line I write, I'm steadily growing.
In the end, I'm gonna wear a crown.
From Duval to Cobb, I'm writing my truth.
I'll take you on a journey with the flow of my ink.
So, come along and join my show.
Let's sing and dance until we are anew.

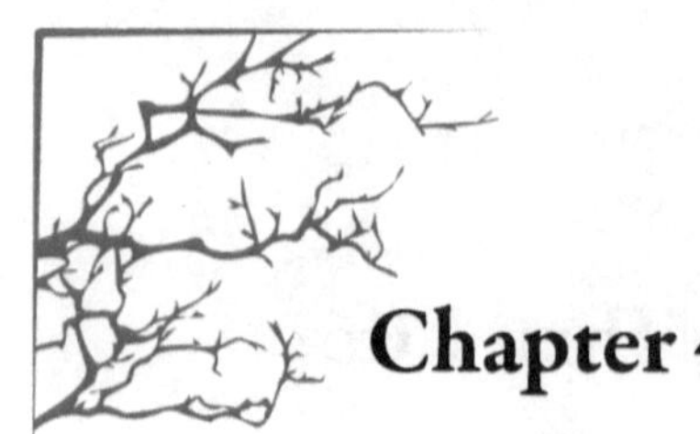

Chapter 41: I've Been There

I'VE BEEN WHERE THE darkness and I meet on the edge of my sanity.

I've been where the shadows taunt me.

They still scream so loudly when I bleed.

I've already been through Hell.

You will never break me!

I'm coming out of my shell, and you will never steal my peace ever again.

I've also been where the darkness meets me at the height of my fucking clarity.

So, just leave me to be me.

Just let me fly free.

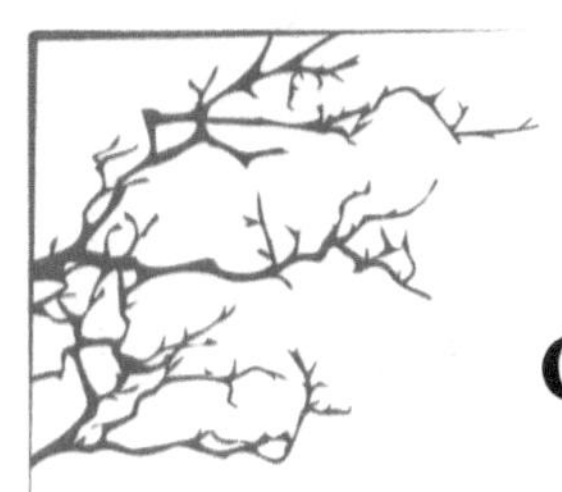

Chapter 42: Motions

JUST GOING THROUGH the motions of being alive,
    not really living, frozen inside.
    Numb from all this pain coursing through my veins.
    Terrified of never escaping the gray,
    watching as my life just fades away.
    Reaching out from the depths of my hell,
    trying to move on,
    but I'm only crawling.
    Soon enough I'll be one of the forgotten,
    lost in myself,
    alone at the bottom.

Chapter 43: Drowning in the Light

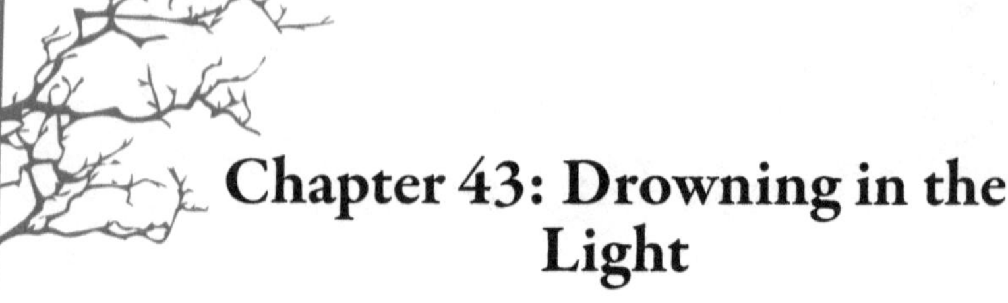

IN THE DARKNESS, I drown in my sorrows.
Tears flow like a river, no peace in sight for me to keep.
The weight of thiworlddt suffocates my soul.
I'm losing control. Beneath the surface, emotions collide.
My heart screams out, but my voice is denied.
I'm trapped in this fight.
Drowning in the light, consumed by the night, silent screams echo in this empty space.
Lost in a sea of pain that I can't erase.
I search for a lifeline but it's nowhere in sight.
Drowning in the light, fading into the night.

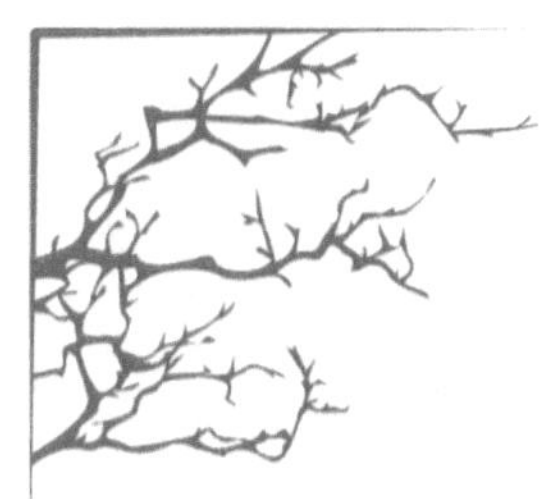

Chapter 44: Dying

SHE WALKS IN DARKENED beauty.
She walks with silent flair.
Strength in every step she takes
as though she owns the air.
She's as deadly as the sharpest blade.
There's no way you could know that she's dying
somewhere deep in her soul.

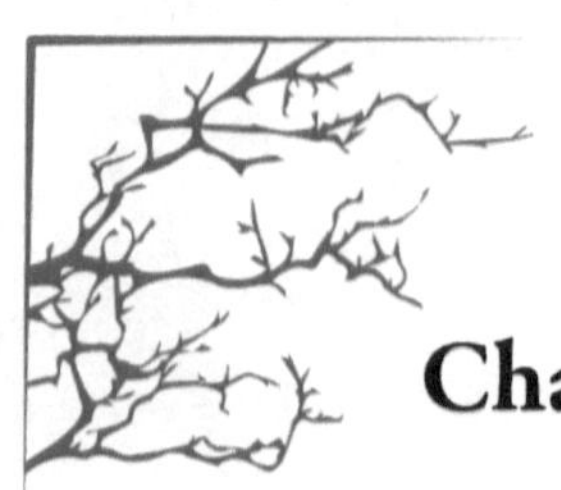

Chapter 45: Tell the Truth

HOW HONEST AM I?
I still won't tell the truth
about how I can't look at you,
without seeing every fucking memory that
I've fought so hard to forget.
I can do it from a distance,
But not face-to-face just yet.
My angels tell me
you don't have any right to know,
but there's that other one
who calls me a coward on the low.
Still, I keep my silence,
better than speaking the truth.
You weren't the villain in my story,
you were just the love I had to lose.

Chapter 46: He Carried You

NOW AT THE CROSSROADS at the stop sign of life,
with only two ways to go- Is it left or right?
In life we have choices, With different options to take.
Will we choose that which is righteous,
Or again opt for a mistake?
So many times in my past I thought I had chosen my own fate,
not knowing God already knew what would happen on that date.
So, if you think you're in control,
Step back and take another look.
He's walked with you hand in hand
through every step you ever took.
When you couldn't walk that's when he carried you.

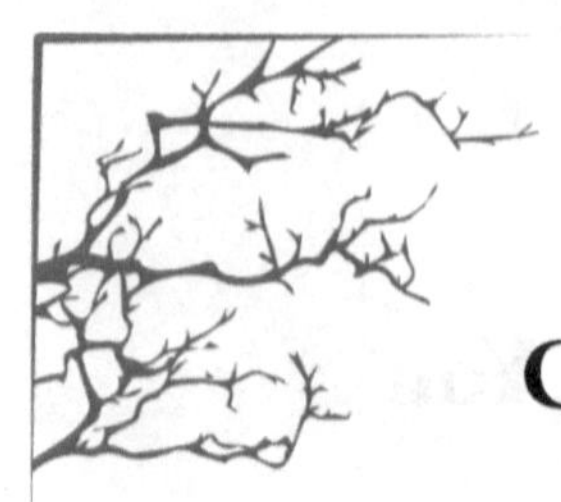

Chapter 47: Different

SHE'S TOO QUIET.
HE'S TOO LOUD.
SHE'S TOO DIFFERENT.
LET'S KEEP THEM OUT.
HE'S TOO SENSITIVE.
SHE'S TOO TOUGH.
HE'S TOO SOMETHING.
WE'RE NEVER QUITE ENOUGH.
WHO CARES IF WE'RE BROKEN, TORN AND TATTERED?
WHO ARE THEY TO DETERMINE WHO MATTERS?
SHE IS PERFECT.
HE'S JUST RIGHT.
DON'T LET GO OF WHO YOU ARE WITHOUT A FIGHT.

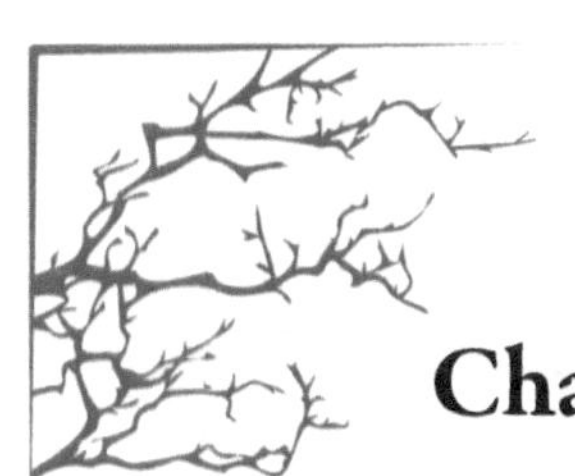

Chapter 48: I'm Damaged

I WON'T BE A PRICE again
    for anyone to pay.
    I know my ass is damaged,
    and I know that's how I'll forever stay.
    My darkness isn't baggage that
    I can just check in at a claims desk.
    I can't leave it cuz I want to,
    it just doesn't work that way.
    I've known myself long enough to know that
    I've gotten really bad.
    I've even spoken with insanity.
    Some souls just never heal.
    Some broken just can't be fixed.
    Some wounds will always bleed.
    So, I refuse to cut another.
    Some blades my soul still needs.

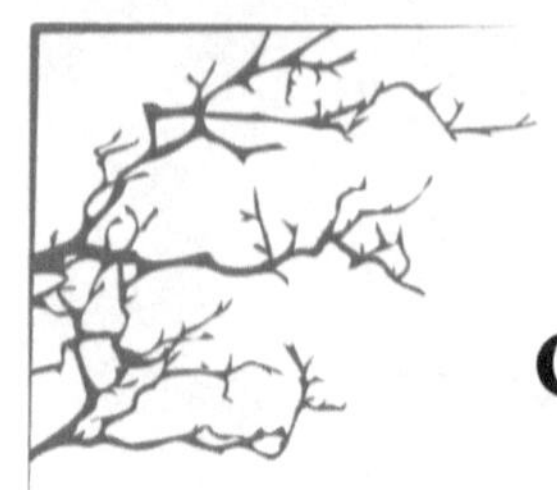

Chapter 49: Rewrote

YOU BURNED THE BOOK.
So, I just rolled and smoked it.
Inhaled the past,
and then rewrote it.
Word after word,
line after line.
You trashed the story,
so, I made it mine.
I told you I'm different,
you were warned from the start.
I'm moonbeams with magick,
I turn pain into art.
I wrote the whole fairytale.
Beginning to end,
then I gave it to the world
so, people could mend
the breaks in their hearts,
their minds, and their souls.
I hope that my story
helps them find their whole.
The rest doesn't matter.
It was all meant to be.
You burned the book
and it became me.
That's how it was written
sometime long ago,
when God made us
and our fates were woven into our souls.

WHISPERS OF THE SOUL

Dust is where we came from
and where we'll someday return.
I've said it for years,
most of us is destined to burn.

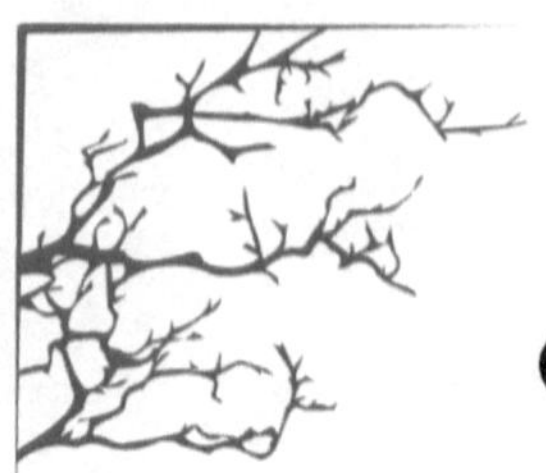

Chapter 50: Aniexty

THERE IS A FEAR DEEP inside that is difficult to define, but it's tearing apart my mind.

It hounds me day and night, drowns out all other thoughts, and turns my life upside down. Anxiety is my stalker, my demise really because it keeps the fear alive while I try to live my life.

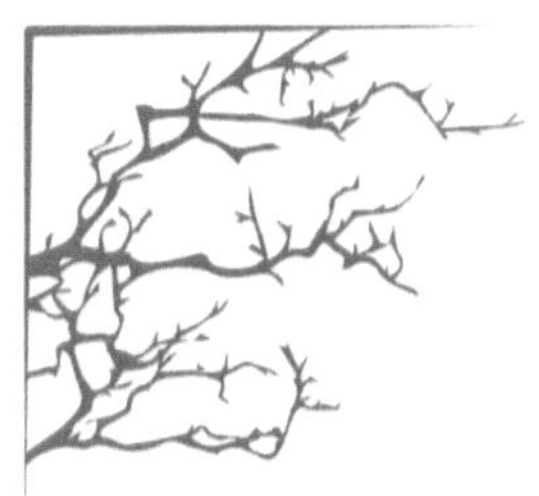

Chapter 51: Fates

FATE FUCKED ME OVER
   when they led me to you.
   They knew I had to lose you,
   so, I'd lose myself, too.
   The pain I had to suffer.
   So many bitter truths, it was
   the only way to level up
   and be able to write the way I do.
   Some say it's a blessing,
   some say it's my strength.
   I grew roses from the heartache.
   Now I'm growing my wings.
   But at the bottom of it all
   there's one thing I can't forget,
   from the moment that we met
   I knew I was just a chess piece
   on a board of bigger things.
   But that knowledge brings no pleasure to the pain built in my
wings.

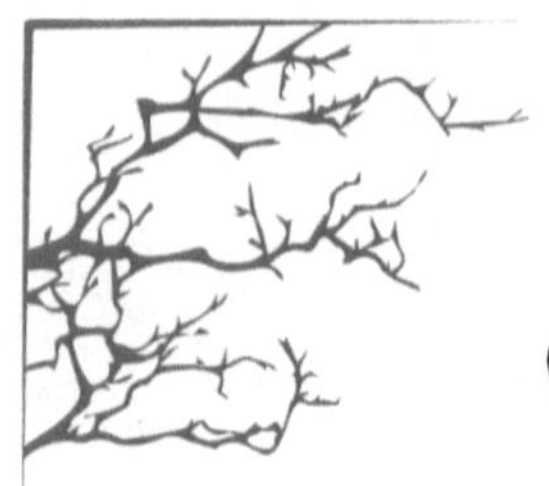

Chapter 52: What if

WHAT IF?
What if on the Other Side,
just 2 questions seal your soul?
What if both your answers
decide which way you go?
What if, to love and to be loved
are the things that make a soul?
And let's say without any answer
you become just an empty shell
to get slung right back into Hell?
What if no one can advance beyond
this level of the game
until they've loved and been loved
and known both sides of the same?
In all things, there is balance,
but this sets the score.
Here is where it gets interesting.
You won't know you've been loved until you're waiting for the chance to move beyond this chessboard and whatever might come next. So, live life like you are Love and you just might pass the test.

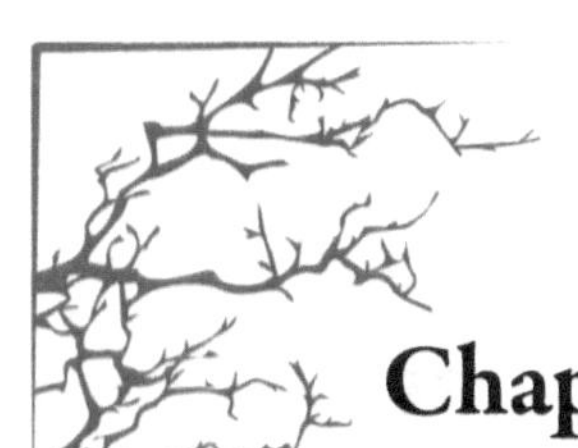

Chapter 53: Tried to Kill Me

WAKING FROM MY SCREAMS yet again,
    the nights, THEY are oh, so fuckin long.
The nightmares, they still exist, you know,
    walls drenched with my blood,
    it seems I never did really escape.
Nowhere's far enough to fuckin run
to get away from all this fuckin pain,
    fuckin anguish and this fuckin fear.
My mind recreates it every damn night,
    as though you're still standing right fuckin here,
    screaming that I'm gonna fuckin die "bitch"
and even explain how you will fuckin kill me and how you will
make sure it damn well will come true, all while the scent of my
blood fills the air as I run the fuck away from you. I hate today, the
anniversary of the day you tried your fuckin best to fucking kill me.
All while you fuckin lied and told me it was fuckin love. 07-01-2001

Chapter 54: Welcome What Floor

I OPEN MY WINDOW AND I sit and display my mind like wind chimes for the breeze to play. Several times today I tried to walk away but I'm called back to this shit like there's something I need to say, but it's not just me, this pen is being led, do you feel it? That something that needs to be said? It's not just about my own thoughts being audible, this writing is a vessel, trying to catch what is possible. So, excuse me if I don't say much, I'm just the elevator operator, Can we lift you up, welcome, what floor? You choose what door do we need to open with these words to unearth what we're working towards. What are we working towards? Something big! Climb into the minds of our hearts. What do we dig up? Staring at this blank page there's so much more to say, every line is like a headstone that rolls down like dominoes, spoken thoughts like street signs, monumental. The spirits I'm hearing are asking for fire; my soul is like a solar system. They are asking me to fan these flames with my attention. Turn my gaze to what sustains, the whole picture, this whole thing. The electricity we hear when we're listening, the live wire, all the blood, the body of the mystery. I can't cease to dream. I'm like a woman coming out of a coma, breathing in all of life, falling in love with life's wonders. I'm a soldier but I no longer carry guns. We are facing a rich man's war with a poor man's blood. A good heart is where it starts, beating like a drum on fire. Mother Earth is a planet, not an empire. The right to raise our voice is different than the ability to be heard. Speak up, don't let others hold you back from what you have to say. The system isn't broken, it was built that way. You can save more lives by taking pens from politicians than guns away from law-abiding citizens. No more lies, no more wars, if opportunity doesn't knock then I'm gonna build a door. A little bit of love can leave a permanent mark, if you like to make this journey take my hand it's time to start. We've been torn apart by race, religion, and blind rage, but that's just a stage as we learn to unite. Now is the time to tell the truth, maybe we can bring some light to this fucked up and dark world.

69

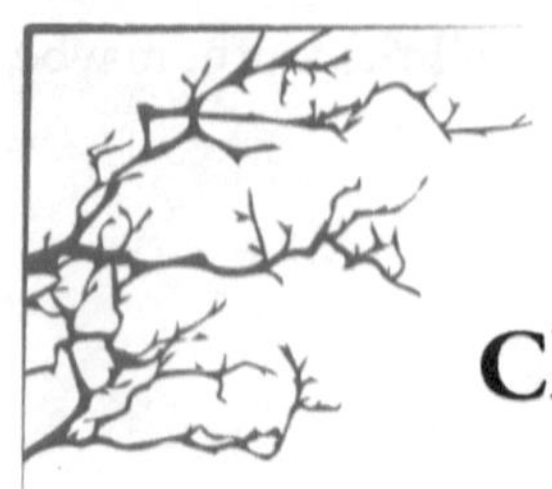

Chapter 55: Just Saying

IT'S MY OBSERVATION.

A lot of people are inspired by darkness. Pain and sadness are their main source of inspiration. They express their pain and suffering in different ways, some with pictures of blood dripping from their bodies from where they had cut themselves to express or help relieve the pain they feel inside.

Why do they do that?

Why do they feed on the pain, and why do they feed the pain?

Do they live such sad, painful lives that it's filled with nothing but suffering?

Clearly, by expressing their pain openly they are actually crying out for help. They feel stuck in a dark, uncomfortable place and they are desperate to get out.

So, why aren't they doing something to find a way of escape?

Why choose to be stuck in the dark?

At the same time, these are the same people who speak of warriors, slaying dragons and demons. Is that their attempt at being positive?

If you wanna express your pain to let off steam, that's fine. But always end it with a positive solution. If not, pretty soon you're gonna run out of masks to wear. FrFr I'm just sayin'!

Chapter 56: Aniexty is a Bitch

MY ENTIRE LIFE HAS been on my mind. Paths I've taken. Mistakes I've made. People I've lost

People I've saved.

I know in the end there will be no one to save me. That's been on my mind too, and for a lot longer than this night.

Melancholy is a terrible lover.

But at least I've lived. At least I've felt love. And at least I've found a way to love myself.

If I had one wish to leave behind, it's that everyone discovers that kind of self-love. The healthy kind. The kind that says I'm worth more than this life tried to give me. The kind that believed in myself when no one else did. The kind that kept me going, even before I knew it existed.

We are all just flashes in time. Moments really. Memories that people will look back on. Finite stars in an infinite sky.

Thanks to my God and the ones that support my writing, my moment just might outlive me. That's all any good writer could ever ask for.

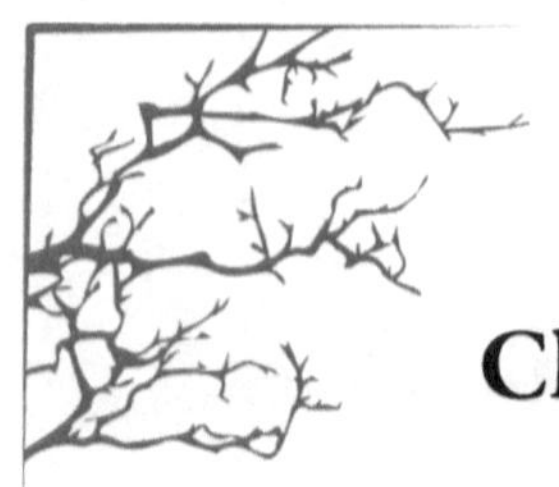

Chapter 57: Thank You

THANK YOU FOR THE GOOD times and thank you for the bad.

Thank you for showing me the strength that I never knew I had.

Thank you for the broken dreams that weren't meant to come true.

Thank you for introducing me to the me left after you.

Thank you for the ending that shattered everything left whole.

But most of all, I thank you for the walls within my soul.

I will never hurt again. Not the way I bled for you. I lined them with explosives so no one could get through. Thank you for the memories, the good and the bad. Last but not least thank you for the love and the heartache that nearly drove me insane but instead left me more than a little mad.

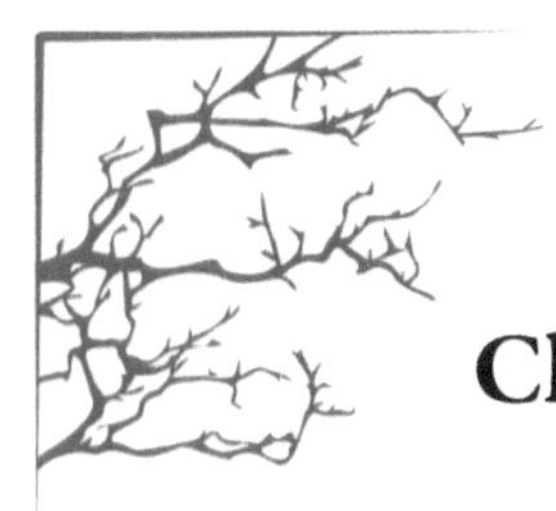

Chapter 58: Beneath the Surface

I GUESS IT'S PAST TIME to open up, just dive right into my pain.

My heart and mind got me tormented, driving me insane.

Scared to die, scared to live, lost in this evil twisted game,

turned to drugs long ago for some peace of mind, but nevertheless,

I know I'm to blame.

Beneath the surface, there lies the truth.

Struggling with demons, I gotta break loose,

gotta change my ways and find a new path.

But please don't judge my journey, cause this shit ain't no fuckin joke.

Real talk, my mind shattered when my heart was abandoned, just left out in the rain, emotionally scarred.

The darkness consumed me, it is ripping me apart,

scared to face the future, shit goes straight to my heart.

Took a wrong turn, and now I'm stuck in this smoke-filled haze.

Drugs were my escape, but it's just dead like me, a phase.

Lost track of time, but I'm ready to be reborn,

gotta fight for my life and give it all that it's fuckin worth.

This life ain't easy, yeah, it sure breaks me down,

but I won't let it define me.

I'm rising from the ashes, gonna seize the day,

No more running away, I gotta find my own way.

Time to reclaim my life, redefine my truth,

no more drowning in despair, seeking only truth.

I'm breaking free from the chains, spread my wings wide,

Leaving pain and heartbreak behind, pushing through this fuckin tide.

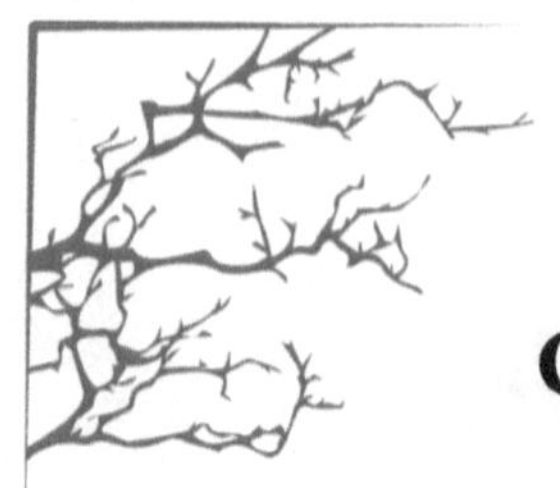

Chapter 59: Reasons

PEOPLE WILL ALWAYS see what they only want to see.

I'm hurting inside that I cannot be who I wanna be.

We all have our good days, and most days are bad.

Some of the words that I hear cut so deep, how can I not feel mad?

Sometimes I try to keep a smile on my face thinking it would help ease my pain.

Almost every day I hear hateful words that make my eyes pour like rain.

So much pent-up anger inside me, it's only a bomb, I'm just waiting for it to explode. I don't have that many friends that's why I'm alone most of the time on life's lonely road. I would complain but it's not like anyone would even fuckin care. I always thought keeping to myself would help in drowning out my fear. Suicidal thoughts are nightmares that I want to forget, but the mystery is I don't even know where the fuck to start. Why should anyone care about me? All I do is give them the reasons to break my heart.

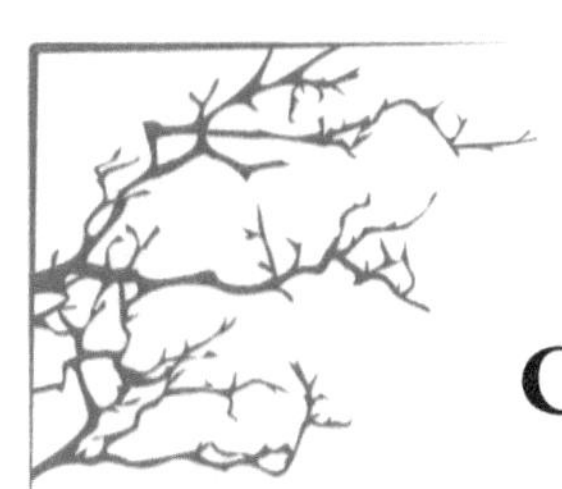

Chapter 60: Fuck You

SOMETIMES SILENCE SAYS more than words could ever say. Intimate with silence most of y'all will never be comfortable with. So, when I give silence, I'm speaking from my soul. It's a part of me.

I've lived with it long enough to know some truths are best
unspoken.
It's my go-to language
when my soul is pouring out its life water,
damaged from whatever or whoever
just shattered my heart again.
Let this be a lesson to you
"Silence speaks my truth",
more than any words could convey,
although usually, it means, "fuck you!"

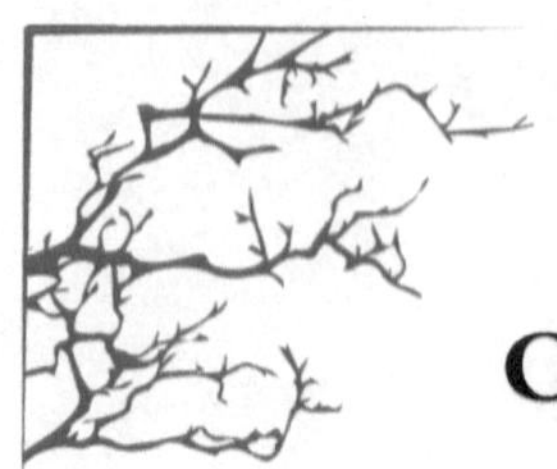

Chapter 61: The Little Murders

THE LITTLE MURDERS, that's what
    I named his words.
    A harmed
    and hurting woman
    is the damage
    that they caused.
    Magazines full of word bullets
    blasting from his lips,
    shooting straight into my chest.
    Gross.
    Useless.
    Worthless.
    Disgusting.
    Stupid.
    Idiot.
    DUMB.
    Ugly,
    Fat,
    Bitch
    Cunt,
    Slut,
    Dog,
    WHORE.
    His words were my little murder.
    For years they were all
    I could see when
    looking in the mirror.

WHISPERS OF THE SOUL

I would hear them
screaming back at me.
Yes, his words were my little murders!
Cutting me right to my soul, unable to ignore the pain, tears would
roll freely down my face.
Plunged sharp spoken knives. Violently screamed, recklessly,
incessantly, until that day when I was finally done.
The little murders, now I no longer hear them when my mirrored
reflection glances back at me. Scars are slowly fading, memories
hopefully erasing.
I AM
still here,
still breathing, still I wake and feel the sun.
Fuck you and your little murderers. I WON!! 04/18/2009

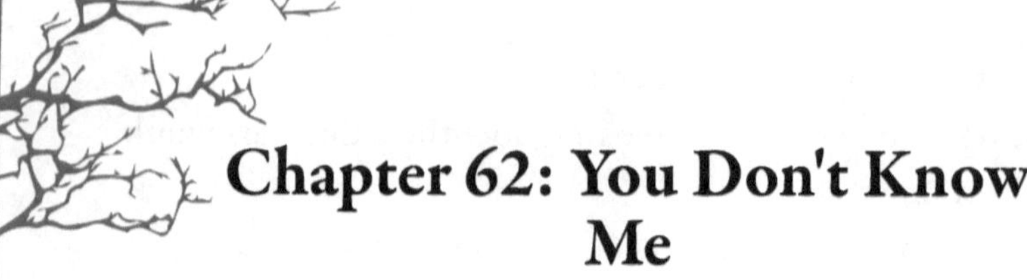

Chapter 62: You Don't Know Me

YOU THINK YOU KNOW me.

You think you've got me figured out.

You don't know the half of it despite the words you spout.

You don't know what I had to literally climb my way out of.

You don't know what nearly buried me,

I've barely survived.

Instead of judging me for who you think I am, how about quit judging me and just trying to give a helping hand?

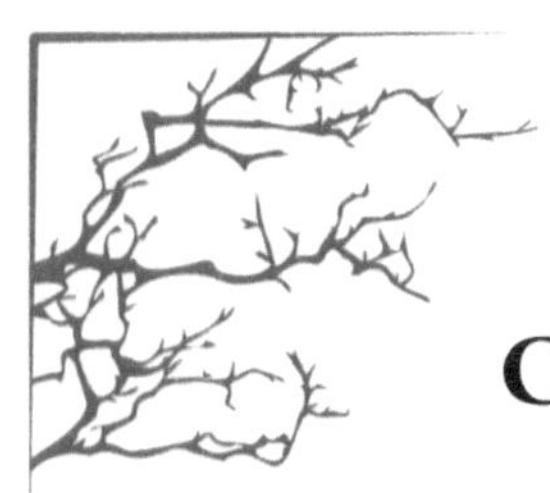

Chapter 63: Too Much

I'M TOLD THAT I'M TOO much to handle. My thoughts are just too heavy to hold. It makes me feel unlovable, carrying this tainted soul. I have the devil inside of me, and most likely I will certainly burn in Hell.

All this just because I suffer from mental health.

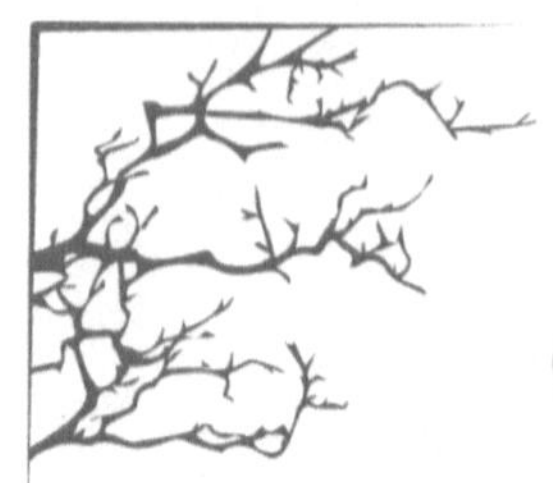

Chapter 64: Miracle

YOU MAY NEVER PERCEIVE the damage hidden in my smiling face,
or how low my spirit really sinks, or how tragic each tear tastes.
You see the put-together, not the pieces that pain takes.
Do you really think she needs to be a masterpiece?
She's a miracle in her own right every single fuckin day!!

Chapter 65: My Haunting Nightmare

WAKING FROM MY SCREAMS yet again,
the nights are oh, so fuckin long.
I still hate this fuckin time of year.
The nightmares, they still exist, you know,
walls drenched with my blood,
it seems I never did really escape.
Nowhere's far enough to fuckin run
to get away from all the fuckin pain,
the fuckin anguish and the fuckin fear.
My mind recreates it every damn night
as though you're standing right the fuck here
screaming that I'm gonna fuckin die "bitch."
and how you will fuckin kill me
and how you will make sure it
damn well, come true,
while the scent of my blood fills the air
as I blindly run the fuck away from you.
I hate this time of year!
The anniversary of the night
you tried you're best to fuckin kill me.
While the whole time you fuckin lied
telling me you loved me.
Now that can't be denied.

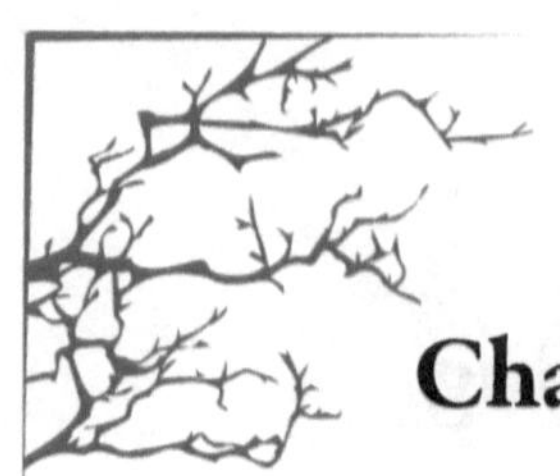

Chapter 66: Prayer to God

TOSS AND TURN, CRASH and burn, every night in my dreams.
It just keeps getting worse, dealing with all this hurt,
at least that's how it seems.
I get so stressed, living like this, each and every day.
That's when I gotta decide to put away my pride
and hit my knees and pray.
God, You are larger than any problems that may arise.
I thank You, Lord,
thank you for allowing me see today's sunrise.
But it's so dark here in my heart.
Please, will You help me out?
Please make it right.
Shine in Your light.

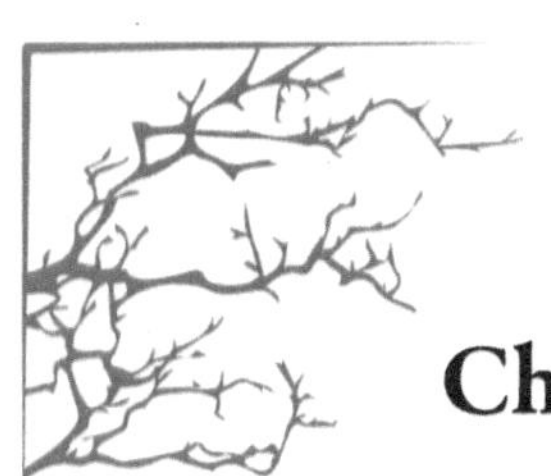

Chapter 67: Eleven Years Gone

I'VE BEEN WALKING THIS road, way too long.
Got this feeling inside, something's all wrong.
Eleven years have passed since you've been gone.
But the pain in my heart, it carries on strong.

Mama, I miss you like it was yesterday.
Though I'm broken, I still need you in every way.
Every tear, every smile, feels like just the other day.
Eleven years gone, but it still feels like yesterday.

Every Sunday morning, without exception,
I used to visit your grave.
But it's your wisdom and your love, I miss.
Through these heartfelt words, the memories pour out.
Because in heartache and longing, they find no cure.

This road of life, sure has taken its toll.
But your spirit lives on, deep within my soul.

I may be shattered, but I won't let go.
Because in my heart, Mama, you'll always grow.

S o, I'll keep singing, keep holding on.
       The love and the memories, they're all I have.
That's what keeps me strong.
Although you're gone, Mama, I'll never be alone.
Because your spirit lives in my heart,
and love for you will forever be shown.
Dedicated to my Mama,
SALLIE ANN ELLISON MORGAN
R.I.P .08/29/2023

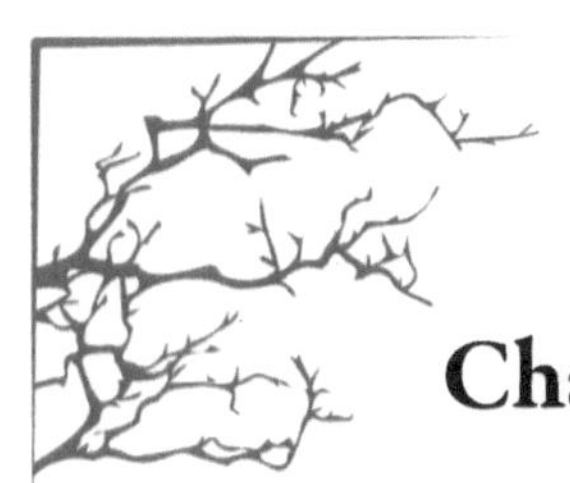

Chapter 68: Running Too

ONCE AGAIN, WE'LL CHASE the sun across the midnight sky,
as if the moon does not reflect that spirit of goodbye.
Like we're not made of chaos.
Although our soul wants it to cease,
we are as out of place as
mermaids in the ravaged Middle East.
Searching for redemption in the remnants of our dreams,
where blood birthed survival in
our nightmares made of screams.
Our life's been made of running, so it's all we know to do,
yet we don't know there's a difference between
"running from" and "running to".
That's the reason that our journey
became a race against the sun.
Instead of finding healing,
we found more reasons left to run,
because that's all we've ever known.
It's how we survived the night.
But now it's time to stop running from
and instead,
run into the light.

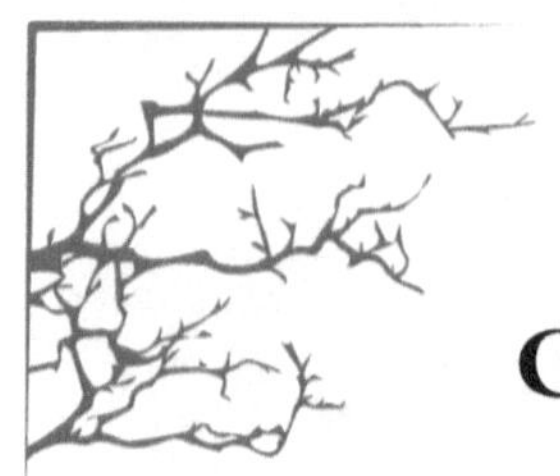

Chapter 69: Queen of Wonderland

WHEN I FIRST CAME TO Wonderland
  I stumbled and boy did I fall and fuckin fast.
  It damn near killed me twice,
  when the worse finally did come to pass.
  But rest assured I'm not your fairytale Alice,
  my other side is so much darker.
  They know now they can't kill me,
  even though they won't stop trying.
  Now I'm fuckin coming for the Queen of Hearts,
  I'mma take that bitch right off her throne.
  I'mma show her who the fuck I am.
  And when the blood stops running
  I'll be the fucking Queen of Wonderland.

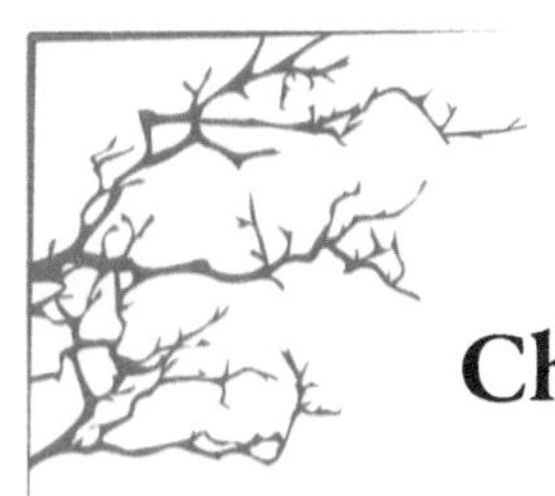

Chapter 70: Question & Answers

I MIGHT BE A POET,

but it's more than what I do.

I don't rhyme because it's easy, but I write because it's true.

My words are more than a story, they paint the life I've lived.

A picture made with only words is all I have left to give.

This life has stolen my heart away,

then it fuckin stole my wonder,

leaving me with only lightning bolts for pens

and ink mixed up with thunder.

The rain, to me, is only grey, there's no color left in it.

Someone gave it to me once and the colors left when they did.

Sometimes, I swear, my ink is blood.

Sometimes it hurts that much

to write of everything I've loved and all I lost,

the wars I've had to fight,

the breaths I've struggled to take when I longed to simply give up.

I know someday I'll win this fight.

It's the one truth we all know.

No one's getting out alive, someday, we all have to go.

When that day does finally come for me,

I just pray I'll have enough left to show others what I've seen,

that all we have is love.

It's the only thing we take with us,

and it's all we leave behind.

It's everything we're made up of.

It's a truth that has no lies.

I know the words I'm writing now won't make sense to everyone,

but they will to those who need
them most just to face another night.
That's why I will never stop writing
till the end so that my words might
find the ones who really need a friend.
Somebody who understands the pain
they hold inside and how they can
never find the words to express the pain
or to help them swim the tide.
Struggling to make it through another day
that only wants to break them.
I'm writing so that they understand,
that sometimes, it's the pain that makes them,
it gives them the strength that others lack,
although they might not see it, right now.
For as warriors, we are born in flames,
no storm could ever drown us.
So, when I finally write my last,
and God takes this pen and takes me home
remember these words, there is help.
I hope and pray I've truly done my mom proud.
Don't forget only love can save you.
I don't mean love from other hearts,
or the kind that makes us glow.
I'm talking of the love inside,
that love that creates you're very soul.

Don't miss out!

Visit the website below and you can sign up to receive emails whenever Sarah EllisonFlake publishes a new book. There's no charge and no obligation.

https://books2read.com/r/B-A-GDRCB-OGPTC

BOOKS 2 READ

Connecting independent readers to independent writers.

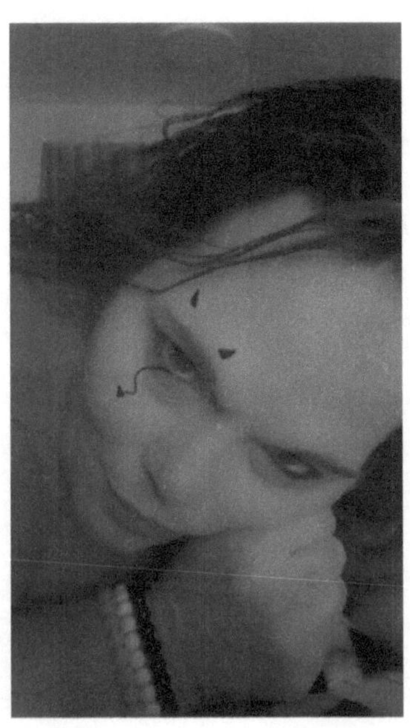

About the Author

Sarah EllisonFlake is a passionate writer who draws inspiration from the various experiences life has thrown her way. At the age of 44, Sarah has weathered many storms, as evident in her heartfelt writings. Hailing from Jacksonville Fla, she currently resides in Georgia. With her focus on capturing life-changing moments from her own life, Sarah's writings will dig deep into your emotions as she shows lessons she's learned along the way. Her unique perspective and raw authenticity make her work relatable to readers from all walks of life.

About the Publisher

First time publisher with a passion for uplifting souls...Kristy Flake is from sunny Jacksonville, Florida and now residing in Georgia. 'Whispers of the Soul is my heartfelt debut, humble words taking you on a journey of resilience, empathy, and healing. Reminding others that they are never alone. Join me on this path of inspiration and support through the power of words. Hopefully, my words are like a hug to you're soul.

Read more at https://sarahellisonflake.wordpress.com.